North Korea

By Charles Piddock

Academic Consultant: Kyung Moon Hwang
Assistant Professor
Department of History
University of Southern California

WORLD ALMANAC® LIBRARY

Please visit our Web site at: www.garethstevens.com
For a free color catalog describing World Almanac® Library's list of high-quality books
and multimedia programs, call 1-800-848-2928 (USA) or 1-800-387-3178 (Canada).
World Almanac® Library's fax: (414) 332-3567

Library of Congress Catalog-in-Publication Data

Piddock, Charles.
   North Korea / by Charles Piddock.
     p. cm. — (Nations in the news)
   Includes bibliographical references and index.
   ISBN-10: 0-8368-6709-2 — ISBN-13: 978-0-8368-6709-1 (lib. bdg.)
   ISBN-10: 0-8368-6716-5 — ISBN-13: 978-0-8368-6716-9 (softcover)
   1. Korea (North)—Juvenile literature. I. Title.
  II. Series: Piddock, Charles. Nations in the news.
  DS932.P54   2007
  951.93—dc22   2006011216

First published in 2007 by
World Almanac® Library
A Member of the WRC Media Family of Companies
330 West Olive Street, Suite 100
Milwaukee, WI 53132 USA

Copyright © 2007 by World Almanac® Library.

A Creative Media Applications, Inc. Production
Writer: Charles Piddock
Design and Production: Alan Barnett, Inc.
Editor: Susan Madoff
Copy Editor: Laurie Lieb
Proofreaders: Laurie Lieb and Donna Drybread
Indexer: Nara Wood
World Almanac® Library editorial direction: Mark J. Sachner
World Almanac® Library editor: Gini Holland
World Almanac® Library art direction: Tammy West
World Almanac® Library editorial production: Jessica Morris

Photo credits: Associated Press: cover photo, pages 5, 8, 11, 12, 13, 14, 15, 18, 29, 32, 35, 36, 37, 38, 39, 41, 42; Landov:
pages 6, 16; The Bridgeman Art Library: pages 20, 22, 23, 26; Alphabet Museum at the JAARS center in Waxhaw, N.C.
painting by Mary Kathleen Greene. Web site: www.jaars.org/museum/alphabet/people/sejong.htm: page 27;
Maps courtesy of Ortelius Design

Printed in the United States of America

1 2 3 4 5 6 7 8 9 10 09 08 07 06

Table of Contents

Cover photo: North Korean soldiers perform during an arts festival at the May Day stadium in Pyongyang, North Korea, in October 2005. The celebration marked the sixtieth anniversary of the ruling Workers' Party of North Korea.

Danger to the World?

In late February 2006, John Negroponte, the head of U.S. intelligence, appeared before the U.S. Senate's Armed Services Committee. He was asked what countries present the most immediate threats to U.S. security. Negroponte singled out two countries: Iran, with its threat to build nuclear weapons, and North Korea. U.S. intelligence, he told the committee, views North Korea with the "highest concern."

"North Korea," he said, "claims to [already] have nuclear weapons—

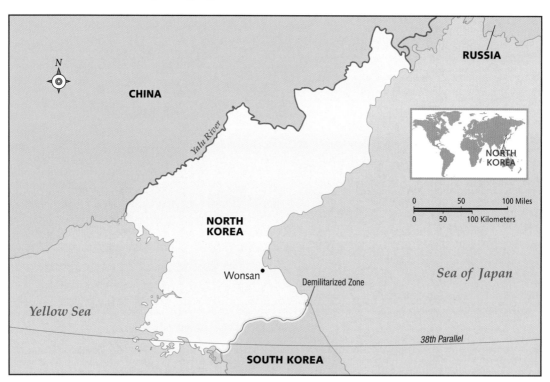

North Korea, with a population of approximately 23 million, is part of the Korean Peninsula. It is bordered by China and Russia to the north and South Korea to the south, Korea Bay and the Yellow Sea to the west, and the Sea of Japan to the east. Pyongyang, the capital, is also its largest city.

A U.S.-led team, along with the Korean Peninsula Energy Development Organization (KEDO), helped build this light water reactor in 2002 as the result of a deal with North Korea. At that time, North Korea agreed to stop development of its nuclear weapons if the United States would provide it with two reactors for electricity.

selling nuclear know-how to other countries and may even have connections to terrorist groups.

"North Korea," Negroponte told another Senate committee, "sells non-nuclear weapons to Africa, Asia and the Middle East" and "has sold ballistic missiles to several Middle Eastern countries." These sales, said the intelligence chief, cause further problems for parts of the world already in conflict.

Negroponte went on to list other U.S. charges against North Korea: that it counterfeits hundreds of millions of U.S. dollars, produces fake American cigarettes and other goods to sell on international markets, and is heavily involved in the world's illegal drug trade.

a claim we assess as probably true—and has threatened to [spread] these weapons abroad." Speaking about North Korea and other nations, Negroponte said, "The potential dangers of [the spread of] weapons of mass destruction ... are so grave that we must do everything possible to discover and disrupt it."

Negroponte was expressing a concern—in the United States and around the world—that North Korea is both armed with nuclear weapons and dangerous to world peace. The United States is worried that North Korea is

History of Bad Feelings

U.S. problems with North Korea are serious, and they are growing more serious as North Korea builds up its nuclear arsenal, but they are not new. The two countries have no diplomatic relations with each other. They see each other as aggressive, a danger to peace, and a world menace. In fact, the United States and North Korea are still official enemies. They fought each other during the Korean War (1950–1953), and a peace treaty formally ending that war has never been signed.

U.S.–North Korean relations have become worse since the mid-1990s.

In 1994, the United States and North Korea were on the verge of war over North Korea's plan to develop nuclear weapons. War was avoided when the Clinton administration signed an agreement to give aid and diplomatic recognition if North Korea stopped developing nuclear weapons. Neither side, however, has followed through with the agreement.

When the Bush administration took office in 2001, U.S.–North Korean relations went from bad to worse.

Words were used between the two countries that are not often heard in the polite world of diplomats. In his 2002 State of the Union address, President George W. Bush said that North Korea is part of an "axis of evil" that threatens world peace. President Bush considers North Korea a "**rogue** state" that does not follow the international rules that other nations follow. Such a state's actions are unpredictable and could endanger world peace. In 2002, Bush said that he "loathed"

Kim Jong-il (1942–)

No matter what one thinks of him, Kim Jong-il (*shown left*) is one of the world's most unusual leaders. At sixty-three, he is said to be secretive and shy. He makes few public speeches and travels little inside or outside of North Korea. When he does travel, it is by car or by special train since he is reportedly afraid of flying.

Kim wears special shoes to make him appear taller than 5 feet 3 inches (160 cm). At his seven-story palace, he enjoys singing on his own karaoke machine and has a collection of more than twenty thousand movies. (His favorites include the horror film *Friday the 13th* and Daffy Duck cartoons.) Before he replaced his father, Kim Il-sung, as North Korean leader, Kim wanted to improve the North Korean film industry. One of his efforts was to kidnap a famous South Korean film director whom he forced to make *Pulgasari*, a North Korean version of the Japanese horror film *Godzilla*.

He reportedly keeps up with international developments through the Internet, and outsiders who have met him say he is extremely well informed about what is happening outside North Korea. In common with many other world leaders, Kim is said to surround himself with loyal supporters who do not dare contradict him.

North Korean leader Kim Jong-il. Bush considers Kim a dictator who starves, imprisons, and brutalizes his people. In response, Kim openly called Bush "an imbecile" and a "tyrant that puts Hitler in the shade."

Beginning in the late 1990s, U.S. spy satellites have recorded evidence that North Korea is actively building uranium enrichment facilities. Uranium is the raw material used to fuel nuclear power plants. It must be enriched, or processed in a special way, to be converted into **plutonium**. Plutonium is the material used to build nuclear weapons.

Rising Tensions

On November 14, 2002, tensions between the United States and North Korea rose dramatically when President Bush ordered a ban on oil shipments to North Korea. The ban would not be lifted, Bush said, until North Korea halted its nuclear weapons program. On December 13, in an act of defiance, North Korea asked the United Nations

(UN) International Atomic Energy Agency (IAEA) to remove seals and surveillance equipment from North Korea's Yongbyon nuclear power plant. The seals had been put on in 1994, when North Korea signed an agreement with the United States to stop developing fuel that could be used to build atomic bombs. On December 27, North Korea expelled IAEA inspectors. It said it now planned to reopen a reprocessing plant that could soon start making weapons-grade plutonium.

On January 10, 2003, North Korea announced it was withdrawing from the Nuclear Nonproliferation Treaty (NPT), which it had signed in 1985. The NPT was created in 1968 because leading nations feared that nuclear weapons would spread and pose a grave threat to world peace. Under the NPT's original rules, those nations with nuclear weapons at the time—the United States, the Soviet Union, China, Great Britain, and France—agreed not to give nuclear weapons or information on how to build them to any other nation. Nonnuclear nations signing the treaty agreed not to build nuclear weapons. Nearly 190 nations have signed the NPT to date. Israel, India, and Pakistan, all of which have nuclear weapons, have not signed the treaty.

On February 24, 2003, North Korea test-fired a missile into the

Sea of Japan between South Korea and Japan. It fired a second missile on March 10. The test-firings were widely considered a way to show both South Korea and Japan that North Korea could deliver nuclear weapons to targets in both countries.

Six-Way Talks

Tense weeks followed the missile firings. On June 9, North Korea frightened the world by announcing that it would build nuclear weapons, "unless the U.S. gives up its hostile [anti-North Korea] policy."

Then, on August 1, 2003, Kim Jong-il agreed to six-way talks about North Korea's nuclear weapons program. The six nations invited to the talks were North Korea, South Korea, the United States, China, Russia, and Japan. The parties met in Beijing, China's capital, for three days, from August 27 to August 29. No agreement was reached. The delegates, however, agreed to meet again. Then, on December 9, 2003, North Korea offered to freeze its nuclear program in return for a list of economic and other **concessions** from the United

Delegates to the six-party talks held in Beijing in 2004 gather for a picture as they make their way into a meeting. Included in this picture, left to right, are U.S. assistant secretary of state James Kelly, South Korean deputy foreign minister Lee Soo-hyuck, Chinese vice foreign minister Wang Yi, North Korean deputy foreign minister Kim Kye Gwan, Japanese chief delegate Mitoji Yabunaka, and Russian ambassador at large Alexander Alexeyev.

States. The United States rejected the offer. President Bush said that North Korea should not just freeze its nuclear weapons program but rather end the program and destroy any weapons it had already made. The parties agreed to meet again in 2004 to work out their differences.

The six nations met again early in 2004 with the same result: no agreement. On September 28, North Korea declared to the world that it had already built nuclear weapons. Speaking before the UN General Assembly, Vice Foreign Minister Choe Su-hon said that the weapons were needed for self-defense against "the U.S. nuclear threat."

More Talks

On February 10, 2005, the North Korean government announced that it planned to pull out of the six-nation talks. North Korea said its decision was partly in response to remarks by U.S. secretary of state Condoleezza Rice. Rice had called North Korea an "outpost of **tyranny**." In response, North Korea called Rice and other U.S. officials "gangsters." Secretary Rice called the North Korean announcement "an unfortunate move…because it only deepens the North Korean isolation from the rest of the [world]."

On July 25, the fourth round of six-nation talks began in Beijing. By August 7, however, the talks had again reached a deadlock and a recess was called. Suddenly there seemed to be a breakthrough. On September 19, in a joint U.S.–North Korean statement, North Korea agreed to give up all its nuclear activities and rejoin the Nuclear Nonproliferation Treaty. The United States said it had no intention of attacking North Korea. The celebration over what was called a "historic" agreement, however, lasted only one day. On September 20, North Korea said it would not scrap its nuclear program until the United States gives it a nuclear reactor to make electricity. The deal was off.

World Concerns

Most military experts do not think North Korea will use its nuclear weapons any time soon. They worry, though, that Kim Jong-il could sell such weapons to other countries or people who might use them—terrorists, for example. "The concern is that North Korea could turn into a kind of nuclear Kmart, where [it] could sell nuclear material to Iran…or, God forbid, to…terrorist organizations," said Jon Wolfsthal of the Carnegie Foundation for International Peace. Other experts fear that a nuclear North Korea will spur the spread of nuclear weapons in Asia. "There will be some [people] who will say, 'If

North Korea has nuclear weapons…
why shouldn't we have [them] as well?,"
said Australian foreign minister
Alexander Downer.

Others say North Korea is simply
using its nuclear claims to gain more
aid from the United States and other
countries. "What [North Koreans]
successfully do is create a new issue to
negotiate over. Let's negotiate about
us coming to the talks. If you give us
concessions, maybe we'll think about
it," said Michael Breen, author of a
biography of Kim Jong-il.

Collapsing Economy

In the background of the international
debate over North Korea's nuclear
program is a tragedy: the collapse
of North Korea's economy and
mass starvation.

When North Korea became a truly
independent nation in 1953, it oper-
ated a **command economy**, or a cen-
trally planned communist economy.
The government made the decisions
about what factories and farms would
produce. A command economy differs
from a **market economy**, like that of
the United States, where what factories produce is determined by what
consumers want to buy.

The planned economy worked well
at first. Many new factories opened
and farms produced large crops after
the devastation of the Korean War. In

the long run, however, this economy
failed to raise people's living standards.
North Korea's economy, already way
behind the economies of its neighbors—South Korea, China, and
Japan—began to collapse by the early
1990s. Factories stood empty. Farms
could barely produce enough food.
The country's **gross national product**
(GNP), at an estimated $18 billion, has
dropped a huge 36 percent since 1989.

Mass Starvation

In 1995, a series of natural disasters
combined with North Korea's economic collapse to create one of the
world's worst famines. The famine
killed nearly 2.5 million people over
three years. For the last ten years,
the **international community** has
stepped in to feed 6.5 million people—a third of North Korea's population. During that time, North Korea
has received more food aid than any
other country in the world, under the
World Food Program.

Despite $1.5 billion in emergency
aid, reports of North Korean families

3 1833 05052 2009

Farmers living along the Taedong River in Chollima, near Pyongyang, shore up its banks to prevent flooding of their crops. Floods along the coast of Kangwon Province in 2001 destroyed much of the farmland in the area, making it hard for the landowners to earn a living.

adding to their diets by collecting grasses, acorns, leaves, and wild roots still persist. At the height of the famine, there were repeated tales of **cannibalism** in the countryside. Lack of healthy food has left a permanent mark on North Korea's surviving children. Experts say the average seven-year-old North Korean is seven inches (18 centimeters) shorter and 20 pounds (9 kilograms) lighter than the average South Korean seven-year-old. According to the UN, 7 percent of North Koreans are starving, 37 percent are malnourished (unable to get the right nutrients to maintain health), 40 percent of children are suffering from lack of growth, and 20 percent are underweight.

During these troubled times, however, North Korea's government has continued to spend money to build up its military and its **arsenal** of weapons, including nuclear weapons.

FAST FACT

In Korea, as in China and Japan, the family name, such as "Kim," is written first, and the individual name, such as "Jong-il" or "Il-sung," is written last. This pattern is just the reverse of the order in which names are written in much of the rest of the world.

CHAPTER 2

Inside the Secret State

No nation today has closed itself off so much from the rest of the world as North Korea. Kim Jong-il's country is so protective of its citizens and way of life that it is widely given the nickname of "the secret state."

The few foreign visitors and tourists who have been there describe North Korea's capital of Pyongyang as a city like no other. It is the only world capital where there is no information about the outside world. Pyongyang has no commercial advertising, no neon lights, no rock or pop music, no international magazines or newspapers. The city has little traffic, few pedestrians, no lively commercial shops, and no normal city noise. To some, the North Korean capital city seems like "an underpopulated

On opening day of the Supreme People's Assembly of North Korea in March 2003, deputies raise their party membership certificates in support of their government.

settlement on a barren planet." At night, Pyongyang does not come any more alive, like Tokyo or New York or Paris. There is only darkness and quiet. "There are no lights and it's absolutely silent. You can hear babies crying from the other side of the river," reported Kate McGeown of the British Broadcasting Corporation, who visited Pyongyang recently.

A daylight trip into the countryside reveals little more. McGeown continued, "To catch a glimpse of North Korean life, travelers must stand up inside a tour bus to see over concrete walls perhaps 8 feet [2.4 meters] high. Barbed wire fencing separates the roads from villages and the brown, dry fields, completely [barren] of trees [that died] long ago. A lone farmer tills the hard earth with a cow, and women walk, balancing bundles on their heads."

Taking photographs from a tour bus is forbidden. To enforce the rule, North Korean soldiers stand every few hundred yards, holding red flags at their sides, to be raised if they see a camera lens or flash reflected in a bus window. (Offenders must surrender their film or their digital cameras to be erased.) Even North Korea's main railway is lined with walls so high that foreign passengers cannot see the countryside.

Passengers in North Korea's airports are carefully screened before

A North Korean man rides through Kim Il-sung Square, named for the founder of North Korea, in Pyongyang in April 2002.

they enter the country. According to Barbara Demick of the *Los Angeles Times*, "In the [Pyongyang] terminal, we waited in line to pass through the x-ray detector. At most airports customs officials look for...drugs or insect-infested fruit. In Pyongyang, they screen for foreign newspapers, transistor radios, mobile telephones, anything that could be used to bring in news of the outside world."

Hero Worship, Korean Style

In the United States, visitors would be startled to see statues and giant posters of President Bush with printed quotes

Kim Il-sung (1912–1994)

On July 8, 1994, when Kim Il-sung (*shown left*) died, a tidal wave of sorrow and grief engulfed North Korea. Kim, who had been a famous **guerrilla** fighter against the Japanese when that country took over Korea in 1910, was more than a beloved leader. He was the only leader that North Korea had ever known. The "Great Leader," as Kim was called before his death, had shaped North Korean life for more than fifty years.

Kim was born near Pyongyang in 1912. His family was opposed to the Japanese occupation and fled to China in 1920. It was there that he became interested in **communism**. As a young man, he joined various anti-Japanese guerrilla groups in northern China, eventually becoming a key member of a group of fighters associated with the Communist Party of China. He fought with this group against the Japanese until 1941, when he escaped from the advancing Japanese to the Soviet Union and became a captain in the Soviet army. At that time, the Soviet Union was at war with Germany, and later with Japan. With the defeat of Japan at the end of World War II, Soviet forces occupied the northern part of Korea.

Kim returned to Korea in September 1945 with the Soviet forces and was installed as head of the Provisional People's Committee in Soviet-occupied northern Korea. The Soviets appointed him to officially head North Korea after they withdrew their forces in 1948.

Kim began the Korean War (1950–1953) in an attempt, which failed, to unify all of Korea under communist rule. After the fighting ended, Kim began rebuilding war-damaged North Korea. He launched a five-year national economic plan with all factories owned by the government and all farming done by collective farms (large farms owned by the government). Much of the economy was based on heavy industry, particularly arms production. Kim also promoted the **Juche** philosophy that guides North Korea today.

Even though Kim Il-sung was a dictator, there seems to be much evidence that he was truly beloved by most North Koreans, who greatly honor his memory today.

from Bush and his father at every turn or to hear music praising Bush from loudspeakers or on the radio. Praising Kim Jong-il and his father, Kim Il-sung, who led communist North Korea from its founding in 1948 until his death, however, is completely normal in North Korea. Pictures, monuments, speeches, and songs constantly remind North Koreans who founded the country and who runs it today.

Before Kim Il-sung died, he had prepared Kim Jong-il to succeed him. In the history of Korean kings, it was normal for a son to succeed his father. When Kim Il-sung died, however, it was the first time that a son succeeded his father as leader in a modern communist country. In 1998, as a lasting tribute, North Korea declared Kim Il-sung the country's "Eternal President." That means that no one, not even Kim Jong-il (who is called "Dear Leader"), can ever hold the office of president again in North Korea. Even in death Kim Il-sung officially runs the country.

Foreign observers have compared the admiration the people of North Korea have for the younger Kim to the worship of a god. At school, North Korean children learn that their "Dear Leader" was born under a double rainbow on Mount Paektu, North Korea's highest mountain. Supposedly, a chorus of singing birds announced that a bright star had appeared in the sky. At Kim Jong-il's recent sixty-third birthday celebration—a national holiday—specially grown red flowers named Kimjongilias bloomed in abundance.

A poster at the annual flower show held in Pyongyang, honoring North Korea's leader, shows Kim Jong-il surrounded by special blooms grown in his honor. The February 2005 show marked Kim's sixty-third birthday and attracted visitors from all over the country.

In Pyongyang, all visitors are expected to buy flowers and place them at the base of the 60-foot (18-m) statue of Kim Il-sung on Mansu Hill, then take off their hats in respect. Many tourists are also taken to the Mongyondae Schoolchildren's Palace, where children sing and dance in honor of Kim Il-sung and Kim Jong-il.

According to Barbara Demick of the *Los Angeles Times,*

On our last day we went to the International Friendship Exhibition, which displays nearly 300,000 gifts to Kim Il-sung and

Kim Jong-il. The place is treated like the holy of the holies; you must cover your shoes with cloth slippers to enter. Flashing red lights on a big map of the world pinpoint the locations of the gift-givers, underscoring how many friends North Korea has....

We padded through the vast corridors, taking in such wonders as a life-size [wax statue] of Kim Il-sung.

Lack of Freedom

On paper, North Korea is a democracy. The government rests with a legislature called the Supreme People's Assembly (SPA). Its 687 members are elected every five years from a single list of candidates. The SPA meets only a few days each year. At that time, it approves decisions already made by the Korean Workers' Party (KWP). All of North Korea's leaders must belong to the KWP. Real control of the government in North Korea lies with leaders of the KWP and the military. The head of the National Defense Commission leads both of these groups. He rules the country through the State Administrative Council.

As of 2006, Kim Jong-il held complete power in North Korea as head of the National Defense Commission, general secretary of the KWP, and supreme commander of the People's Army.

North Korean schoolchildren at Pyongyang's Mangyondae Schoolchildren's Palace play an ancient game called baduk (similar to chess) *beneath ever-present photographs of the country's leaders, Eternal President Kim Il-sung and Dear Leader Kim Jong-il.*

The Korean War was part of a much larger world struggle called the Cold War (1945–1990). The Cold War was a battle for the control of the world between a group of communist nations, led by the Soviet Union, and a group of Western nations, led by the United States. It is called the Cold War because it never developed into a "hot war" between the U.S. and the Soviet Union. Nevertheless, both nations engaged in a nuclear arms race and sponsored smaller nonnuclear conflicts around the world. The Korean War and the Vietnam War (1964–1975) were two such conflicts. Soviet support and encouragement of Kim Il-sung's invasion of South Korea marked the Soviet Union's effort to defeat the United States and its allies in the Cold War. The Soviet Union collapsed into separate countries in 1991.

Almost everyone outside North Korea agrees that North Koreans really have no rights at all. The press is controlled by the government; free speech is not allowed. There is no freedom of religion, even though some temples remain open with a few monks as a show for tourists. North Koreans cannot leave the country or freely move about within it. For this reason, few North Koreans are allowed to buy cars or bicycles, even if they can afford such luxuries.

Political Prisoners

Human Rights Watch, an international group that monitors human rights abuses, estimates that 200,000 political prisoners are held in isolated camps throughout North Korea. Entire families have been imprisoned together. They undergo "**reeducation**" until they die or convince prison officials that they

have become faithful followers of Kim Jong-il. Ninety-five percent of the people who go into prison in North Korea die there. Bradley Martin, author of *Under the Loving Care of the Fatherly*

FAST FACT

The Korean Peninsula has been called "the scariest place on earth" by some visitors. The reputation comes from the size of the armed forces of both Korean states and North Korea's development of nuclear weapons. North Korea, whose population is almost 23 million, has the world's fourth-largest military force, with about 1.1 million soldiers, sailors, and air crews. Another 4.7 million North Koreans are in the reserves, with an additional 3.5 million in a military group called the Red Guards. All males between the ages of sixteen and twenty-eight are required to serve between three and ten years in the military. North Korea spends an estimated 12 to 44 percent of its gross national product on its military. The average for the rest of the world is about 2.6 percent.

Leader, a recent book on North Korea, calls it the most repressive and brutal country in the world today. Martin tells of whole families sometimes executed if one member slights Kim Jong-il.

Park Choong-il, one of the rare prisoners to escape from a North Korean prison, described conditions to Life Funds for North Korean Refugees, a group opposed to the regime of Kim Jong-il. Park was arrested for trying to flee from North Korea to South Korea in 1999:

> I was taken to...underground cells beneath the building...a corridor divided cells for men and cells for women. There were a total of 12 cells on the men's side. There was only a dim light from a single bulb in the cell, and no sunlight.... The cells were full of lice, bedbugs, fleas and other insects.... Prisoners received three meals a day, a very small quantity of hardboiled corn and very thin salt soup. We were never allowed to speak and move around in the cell.

Park also described regular torture and the screams of those tortured. He was able to escape after being released by an uncle who had connections with the government.

Self-Reliance

Communism is an economic and political system that is often stated to be the idea on which North Korea's society is based. Communism says that

At a press conference held in Los Angeles, California, in 2003, two North Korean refugees talk about the years of abuse they endured as prisoners in a North Korean prison camp. Yung Kim (center) and Min Bok Lee (right) are joined by interpreter and peace activist Douglas Shin in an attempt to encourage film director Steven Spielberg to make a movie publicizing the horrors in their homeland.

Compared to North Korea, South Korea today is a strong example of the difference between a communist and a capitalist economy and political system. Capitalist South Korea is an economic dynamo, one of the world's most powerful economies. A functioning democracy with a relatively free press, South Korea is one of Asia's richest nations. Its living standards are much higher than those of North Korea, and its per capita GNP is roughly twenty times that of North Korea.

Until the 1990s, however, South Korea suffered from a series of dictatorial governments and was plagued by student and worker unrest. Nevertheless, during the eighteen-year dictatorship of Park Chung-hee, the nation experienced rapid economic growth. When Park was assassinated in 1979, General Chun Doo-hwan seized power. Massive student demonstrations in 1980 resulted in a military crackdown with much loss of life. Still more unrest forced Chun from power in 1988. Since then, South Korea has become more democratic and more prosperous. Its current president, Roh Moo-Hyun, was elected in 2002.

all property should be owned by the state, which represents the people. Profits and income should be shared equally by all. Communists argue that capitalism, under which property is privately owned and profits are not shared equally, is unfair to workers.

In today's North Korea, however, the more powerful guiding belief is Juche (joo-CHEE), a Korean form of self-reliance. Juche means that North Koreans should work to be politically, militarily, and economically self-supporting. Juche believers agree that Kim Jong-il can lead the country toward complete self-reliance. The belief in Juche is why North Korea refuses to be dominated by more powerful nations, such as China and Japan, who have controlled Korean governments in the past. Juche has led North Korea to defy the United States and to refuse badly needed aid, even in the face of famine. Juche is also a strong influence in North Korea's development of nuclear weapons despite objections by the United States and other nations.

Juche is also a chief reason for North Korea's isolation from the rest of the world. North Korea's only allies were the fellow communist nations of the Soviet Union and China. When China began trade and diplomatic relations with noncommunist, capitalistic South Korea, and the Soviet Union collapsed, North Korea became truly isolated.

CHAPTER 3

"Land of the Morning Calm"

Long before there was a North Korea or a South Korea, ancient peoples lived in the Korean Peninsula. One of the names they called their mountainous land was Joseon (jo-SEE-ahn), or "Land of the Morning Calm." The name comes from the way the land looks in the early morning when the mists from the night still hover in the mountains and forests, giving a calm and peaceful feeling.

Gojoseon ("ancient" Joseon) was the first Korean kingdom. According to legend, it was founded in 2333 B.C. by Dangun, grandson of the king of heaven. Gojoseon was located between the Liao River, just north of the present-day border between North Korea and China, and the Daedong River in present-day North Korea. The people of Gojoseon, the ancestors of today's Korean people, were related not to the Chinese to the north or to the Japanese to the southeast, but to the people of Central Asia. When they migrated from

A drawing of Dangun, the legendary founder of Korea, who built the city of Pyongyang.

According to Korean legend, King Dangun is the founder of Korea and the father of the Korean people. His father was Hwanung, the son of the ruler of Heaven. Dangun's mother had once been a bear before Hwanung transformed her into a human being. The legend says that King Dangun was born near Mount Paektu. On what is now October 3, in 2333 B.C., Dangun moved to Pyongyang, where he built a walled city and established the ancient Gojoseon kingdom. From that year, Koreans mark five thousand years of history. Today, North Koreans and South Koreans celebrate October 3 as National Foundation Day. Dangun is supposed to have lived more than one thousand years before he became a mountain god in far northern Korea.

Central Asia to the Korean Peninsula is not known.

Ancient Gojoseon developed the use of iron, an improvement on weaker bronze, and made iron daggers and spears beginning about 300 B.C. Gojoseon also developed advances such as the *ondol* method of using pipes to heat a house by circulating kitchen heat from room to room under the floorboards. The method continues to be used in Korea today.

Enter the Chinese

Unfortunately for the people of Gojoseon, Korea then, as today, lay between much larger countries that often wanted to control the Korean Peninsula. In 109 B.C. Emperor Wudi of the Han **dynasty** in China ordered his armies to begin a massive invasion of Gojoseon. A year of heavy fighting ensued, but by 108, Pyongyang, the Gojoseon capital, fell to the Han army. Korea became part of the Han Empire. The Chinese divided up Gojoseon into four territories. Each territory sent yearly gifts in the form of crops and other goods to China. The Gojoseon rulers were kept in office, but they had to send gifts to the Han emperor.

During the time Korea was ruled by the Han emperors, many Chinese scholars came to Korea. A wide cultural exchange resulted between the Chinese and the Koreans. Chinese ways of thought and culture came to heavily influence the Koreans. The Gojoseon Koreans had no written language, so they changed the complex Chinese writing system to express the Korean language. They also were influenced by two new religions that came to them from China: **Confucianism** and **Buddhism**. Both helped shape the development of Korean culture and continue to influence Korean civilization today.

Confucianism was based on an ordered society where natural loyalties and obedience to wise rulers were followed. Buddhism, begun in India and now a major world religion, places importance on compassion and spiritual equality. Both systems of belief helped create a stable, productive society in ancient Korea. Both also greatly influenced education and the arts.

A silk wall hanging shows an ancient leader inviting a scholar of Confucianism into his home to help him study the honored religion.

Buddhism was founded in India by the spiritual teacher Siddhartha Gautama (*shown left*) about 528 B.C. Born a prince, Siddhartha gave up his throne in order to seek the true meaning of life. After meditating under a tree, he achieved self-knowledge, or enlightenment, at the age of thirty-five. He became known as the Buddha, or the Enlightened One. He then began a lifelong effort to teach others the true path to enlightenment. He died at age eighty. His final words were, "All composite things pass away. Strive for your own salvation with diligence."

After the Buddha's death, his followers multiplied and Buddhism grew in influence in India and throughout southern Asia. It also split into a number of schools and divisions, each with its own way of thinking about the Buddha's teachings. The religion entered Korea from China in the fourth century A.D. It became the state religion in each of the Three Kingdoms, in unified Silla, and in the Goryeo kingdom. In the mid-1900s, however, many Koreans came to think that Buddhism was old-fashioned, and Christianity grew in popularity. In North Korea, the government took over the Buddhist temples and now uses them for nonreligious purposes. In recent years, however, the North Korean government has allowed the establishment of a Buddhist academy and services in a few temples. In South Korea, Buddhism remains a strong force and the religion of the majority of the people.

The Three Kingdoms

China's direct rule of the Korean Peninsula soon began to weaken. Although gifts were still given each year to the Chinese emperor, by 37 B.C. native Korean rulers were in direct control of most of Korea. The peninsula was divided into three Korean kingdoms: Goguryeo, Silla, and Baekje. By the 500s A.D. all Three Kingdoms had well-established territories with prosperous cities, advanced schools of Confucian thought, and well-established Buddhist temples. Buddhism became the state religion for all three.

Goguryeo, Silla, and Baekje were in a near-constant state of war with

Confucianism

Confucianism is not strictly a religion as is Buddhism or Christianity. In Confucianism, there are no priests or monks, no god, no churches, and no worship. Instead, Confucianism is a system of relationships with a code of behavior. This system was developed by Kong Fuzi ("Master Kong"), or Confucius, a Chinese teacher and philosopher who lived between 551 and 479 B.C.

After working for the government, but seeing no improvement in its rule, Confucius resigned as the justice minister at age fifty. He then began a twelve-year journey around China, looking for a way to create good government and an ordered, productive society. He spent the last years of his life teaching an increasing number of people who believed in the same things he did. He wrote a number of books, including the set of books called the Five Classics. After his death, the wisdom of Confucius was put into a book called the Analects.

According to Confucius, there were five ranks of relationships, such as ruler and subject or parent and child. In each relationship, the weaker or younger person submits to the stronger or older one, and the stronger person protects the weaker one. Between friends, there is equality, but that is only if the two persons are the same age and gender. Respect for one's elders led to respect for ancestors. Thus, Confucianism called for special ceremonies of ancestor worship. In addition, Confucianism required that government officials be scholars who had passed a difficult test. To prepare for this test, young men spent years studying in Confucian schools.

Historians believe that Confucianism was in Korea before A.D. 1000. Later, it became the official philosophy or state religion of the Joseon dynasty (1392–1910). The long history of Confucianism in Korea has shaped Korean society. Koreans respect their parents and honor their ancestors. The leaders of North Korea have benefited from Confucianism in building the loyalty of their people. Confucianism has also helped create a strong sense of community and self-reliance. When times get tough, Koreans stick together. Juche, North Korea's idea of extreme self-reliance, fits well within the Confucian tradition.

each other. In 660 Silla formed an alliance with China's Tang Dynasty. With the help of a Tang army, Silla conquered both Baekje and Goguryeo to form a united Korea. Then, a few years after uniting the country, the Silla army pushed the Tang army out of Korea and back into China. From 668 to 918, Silla controlled all of Korea. The Silla kings ruled from their capital, Gyeongju, now in South Korea.

The Silla and Goryeo Kings

The Silla kings supported a very rigid system of rank in Korean society called the bone rank system. This system of rating heredity was used to rank Korean aristocrats based on their closeness to the throne. Introduced by King Beopheung in 520, bone rank determined the status of a family, from the size of its home to the clothing and number of things it could own. Bone rank also determined how high an office in the government one could hold.

The highest bone rank was "hallowed bone," which applied to part of the royal Kim family. Only those with this rank were permitted to be king. Just below hallowed bone was the rank of "true bone." True bone included the rest of the royal family plus several other high aristocratic families. Below true bone were a number of lesser bone ranks.

Korea generally prospered under the Silla Dynasty. In the 700s the kingdom reached its height. Gyeongju had many great and wealthy Buddhist temples. The Silla kings built a great palace in Gyeongju in a green valley with majestic mountains rising on each side.

In the 800s, however, the Silla kingdom began to decline. Aristocrats tried to limit the king's power, and overtaxed peasants revolted. In 918, general Wang Geon ended Silla rule. He established a new dynasty, the Goryeo Dynasty, with its capital at Gaeseong. The modern name *Korea* comes from the name *Goryeo*. Wang married a woman from the Silla family and ruled the entire Korean Peninsula from the southern tip to the Yalu River, today's border between North Korea and China.

The Goryeo kings abolished bone rank and, under the supervision of Confucian scholars, made knowledge, not heredity, the road to advancement in Korean society and government. As in China, civil servants had to pass a series of very tough examinations to rise in the ranks. In the 900s, Buddhism became the official state religion.

Mongol Domination

In the early 1200s, a storm was brewing in Central Asia that would burst upon all the countries of Asia and Europe with untold violence. The **Mongols** rode out of Mongolia and terrified the known world. These wild horsemen of north Central Asia fought like demons and killed without

Kublai Khan, wearing a white robe with black collar and cuffs, is surrounded by members of his royal court.

mercy. Once united, disciplined, and organized under a military genius named Genghis Khan, Mongol armies conquered nearly all of Asia and much of eastern Europe.

When Genghis died in 1227, his son Ogodei became the ruler of the Mongol Empire, which stretched from China to the borders of Poland. In 1231, Ogodei sent a Mongol army into Korea to punish the Goryeo king for not giving his yearly gift. In 1232,

the Koreans revolted against Mongol domination, beginning a tough, hard-fought, and bloody war that would last for decades. It took the Mongols until 1259 to complete the conquest of Korea. The Goryeo kings still officially remained rulers of Korea, but they were subject to the Mongols.

Ogodei was succeeded in China by Genghis Khan's grandson, Kublai Khan, who founded the Yuan Dynasty (1260–1368). After consolidating his rule in China, Kublai Khan sent envoys to demand gifts from the Japanese. Insisting that they were not subject to his rule, the Japanese prepared for war. In 1274, Kublai launched a massive sea assault—with up to nine hundred ships and twenty-three thousand troops—on Japan from southern Korea, but bad weather forced the fleet back. In 1281, the great Khan ordered an even more massive invasion of Japan, this time with four thousand ships. As before, many Koreans were forced to take part in the expedition.

For fifty-three days, the Japanese, led by samurai warriors, held off the huge Mongol army on a narrow beach on the island of Kyushu. Then a hurricane struck, destroying half the Mongol fleet and forcing the invaders to leave. The Japanese interpreted the hurricane as a *kamikaze*, or "god-wind," that saved Japan.

The Joseon Dynasty

Mongol power in Korea was in steady decline by the late 1300s. In 1388, the Goryeo king ordered General Yi Seong-gye to attack a Chinese province. Instead, the general overthrew the king and seized power. In 1392, Yi himself was proclaimed king, establishing the Joseon Dynasty (1392–1910), named after the ancient name for Korea. Yi moved his capital

to Seoul and made Confucianism the state religion, replacing Buddhism.

Yi's grandson, King Sejong (1397–1450), is today regarded as Korea's greatest ruler. He extended the Korean border in the north to the Yalu and Tumen Rivers. This is North Korea's northern border today. He

King Sejong of Korea was a man of great vision who, among other accomplishments, created a system of justice that barred cruel punishment for criminals and guaranteed a person numerous trials before being condemned.

The Korean Language

The Korean language is not related to either the Chinese or the Japanese language. It is part of the Altaic-Turkic language group of Central Asia. During the 1400s, King Sejong ordered his scholars to create a new alphabet for the Korean language. Previously, Koreans used Chinese characters to express their thoughts on paper. The Chinese written language, however, had thousands of characters, with a separate character for each idea. This system made it very hard to learn to write Korean, so only scholars were able to read and write.

Sejong wanted more of the Korean people to be literate, so he ordered his scholars to find a simpler alphabet. In response, the scholars developed the hangeul alphabet. In 1446, they presented King Sejong with the new alphabet in a document called *hunmingeongeum*, which means "correct sounds for the instruction of the people." The new alphabet had ten vowels and fourteen consonants. It was a phonetic alphabet, with each letter having its own distinct sound. That made it easier to put letters together in many combinations to form a large vocabulary of written words.

At first, only the common people used hangeul. Scholars continued to use Chinese characters. Only after World War II did hangeul become the official system for writing Korean. On October 9 each year, South Korea celebrates Hangeul Day in honor of the invention of the alphabet in 1446.

encouraged inventions such as the rain gauge, the use of movable type, and the creation of a Korean alphabet called **hangeul**, still in use today.

Korea, however, continued to be plagued by its position between the two large powers of China and Japan. In 1592, Japanese forces invaded Korea on their way to attack China, which was then ruled by the Ming emperors. The Japanese army landed at Pusan, now Korea's second-largest city, and captured Seoul and then most of the peninsula. In response, the

Ming army united with the Koreans to force the Japanese out of Korea. Japan made another attempt to conquer Korea in 1598, but did not succeed. The war, however, greatly damaged Korea. Thousands of people were killed, cities were ruined, and farmland lay uncultivated.

After recovering from the Japanese invasions, Korea was invaded again in 1627 and in 1636 by the Manchus, who ruled Manchuria just north of Korea. The Joseon army surrendered to the Manchu army. Korea now sent gifts to the Manchus, who soon controlled all of China as well. In response to the Manchu invasions, the Joseon Dynasty closed Korea off to all countries except China. Between the 1640s and the late 1800s, Korea kept itself so apart from the rest of the world that it became known as the Hermit Kingdom.

Japanese Dominiation

In 1876, however, Korea began to open up to the world when it was forced by Japan to sign the Ganghwa Treaty. The treaty opened the port cities of Pusan, Inchon, and Wonsan to trade with Japan. In 1882, the United States signed a similar treaty with Korea, and within a few years a number of European nations also signed trade treaties.

At the end of the 1800s, Korea's neighbors—China, Japan, and Russia—tried to gain control of the Korean Peninsula. In 1894 and 1895, Japan fought China for influence in Korea. Japan easily won the war and forced China to recognize Korea as an independent country. For the first time in two thousand years, Korean rulers no longer had to pay tribute to a ruler in China. A few years later, in 1904–1905, Japan defeated Russia in the Russo-Japanese War. One result

Japanese troops wait to cross a river near Ping Yang, Korea, during the war between Russia and Japan for Korea in 1904.

of the war was that Korea was now officially declared to be under Japanese "protection." Only five years later, in 1910, Korea became a colony of Japan. The last Joseon king, Sungjong, was forced to give up his throne and move to Japan.

Japanese Rule

Japan ruled Korea from 1910 to 1945. It was not a happy time for Koreans. Japan's government brought Japanese farmers and workers to Korea to resettle. Japan divided the entire peninsula into a southern agricultural area and a northern industrial and mining area—divisions that even today help form the economies of North Korea and South Korea.

The Japanese also attacked Korean culture. In schools, they replaced the use of the Korean written and spoken language with Japanese. Korean history was no longer taught. The Japanese even replaced Korean names with Japanese names.

In response to this cultural war, many thousands of Koreans fled the country to live in China, Russia, and the Hawaiian Islands. Discontent with Japanese rule was so high among Koreans that they signed a "declaration of independence" that was read aloud on the streets of Seoul on March 1, 1919. Thousands of people peacefully rallied for independence.

The Japanese brutally put down the protests, killing an estimated seven thousand Koreans.

In the 1930s, Japan was at war with China. To support its war effort, Japan forced thousands of Korean men and boys to serve in the Japanese army. Other Koreans were forced to go to Japan to work on farms or in factories. When Japan became involved in World War II (1939–1945), thousands more Koreans were forced to sacrifice themselves for the Japanese war effort.

Birth of North and South Korea

With the defeat of Japan in 1945, the Allies (the United States, Soviet Union, and Great Britain) agreed to divide the Korean Peninsula between the Soviet Union and the United States at the thirty-eighth parallel as a temporary measure. Soviet troops marched into Korea north of the parallel and accepted the surrender of Japanese troops there. South of the thirty-eighth parallel, U.S. forces accepted the surrender of Japanese troops.

Immediately, however, Soviet forces closed off northern Korea at the thirty-eighth parallel and placed Korean communists in power there. One of those men was a guerrilla fighter who had fought the Japanese during the war: Kim Il-sung. Kim was elected secretary of the North Korean

Communist Party and chair of the temporary government in the north. In the south, the government was run by the U.S. military. In 1946, the Americans set up the Representative Democratic Council, headed by Syngman Rhee.

In 1948, UN-supervised elections were supposed to take place in both the north and south parts of Korea to choose a national assembly to rule the entire country, but the Soviets refused to allow UN officials to enter the north. In May 1948, elections were held in the south, and a National Assembly was elected, a constitution adopted, and a government formed. Syngman Rhee was elected president of South Korea in July 1948, and in August the Republic of Korea was proclaimed.

In the north, the Supreme People's Assembly was formed, with Kim Il-sung appointed as premier. In September 1948, the Democratic People's Republic of Korea was established in the north. In 1949, the Soviet Union and the United States withdrew their troops from the Korean Peninsula. The Soviets left behind a well-equipped, well-trained North Korean army of 135,000 men, supported by tanks and artillery.

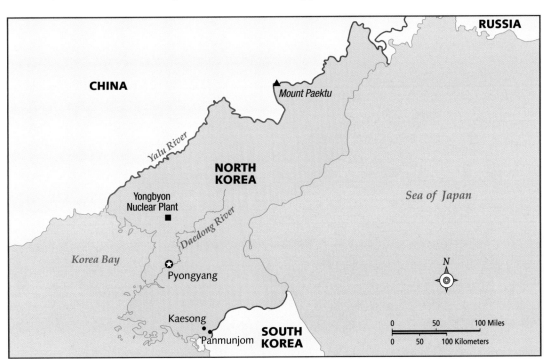

This map of North Korea shows the location of North Korea's nuclear facility at Yongbyon, 62 miles (100 km) north of Pyongyang. The plant was built in 1964 with help from the Soviet Union. In 2002, North Korea asked the IAEA to remove its seals and cameras within the facility. The international community believes the plant has produced enough fuel for eight to eleven nuclear weapons.

CHAPTER 4

The Korean War

On June 25, 1950, Kim Il-sung ordered his army to cross the thirty-eighth parallel and invade South Korea. The well-armed North Korean army swept southward, overwhelming all opposition.

South Korea and its allies were caught by surprise. U.S. troops stationed in Japan were quickly shipped to Korea. South Korean troops and their U.S. allies, however, were defeated and pushed south by the

Refugees from South Korea, fleeing advancing communist troops in January 1951, cross a land bridge that stretches across rice paddies toward their destination of southwestern Korea, where they will be transported to an island refugee camp.

northern army. On the same day, the UN Security Council, in an emergency meeting, voted to demand that North Korea stop its attack and return to its borders. North Korea ignored the demand. The UN then sent troops from many countries to act as a single international force.

On June 29, Seoul, South Korea's capital, fell to the North Koreans. Still, Kim Il-sung's army pushed southward, driving U.S. and South Korean forces into rapid retreat. By the end of July, the northern army had pushed U.S. and South Korean troops to the tip of Korea around the city of Pusan. The U.S. Eighth Army commander, General Walton Walker, tried to rally the UN troops. He delivered a famous "stand or die" speech, saying that the UN force could no longer retreat. The defenders dug in and fought off one furious attack after another. They awaited reinforcements and orders by the new commander in Korea, General Douglas MacArthur. It seemed to the United States that the war was lost and that Kim had quickly achieved his goal of uniting Korea under communist rule.

The Inchon Landing

While U.S. and other UN troops continued to fight at Pusan to hold off the advancing North Koreans, General MacArthur devised a bold plan. He sent troops by sea to the port of Inchon, near Seoul. By landing at Inchon, 150 miles (241 kilometers) behind North Korean lines, MacArthur figured that he could attack the enemy from the rear, turning defeat into victory.

On September 15, 1950, Joint Task Force Seven, with more than 320 warships, including four aircraft carriers, transported seventy thousand American marines and other troops into Inchon harbor. Preceded by a heavy bombardment of naval guns and waves of fighting aircraft, the First Marine Division landed at Inchon, totally surprising the North Koreans. Although it had seemed as if South Korea would lose the war only two months before, it now appeared that it would win. Their communications cut and under heavy bombardment, the North Koreans broke and fled back north across the thirty-eighth parallel. U.S. forces retook Seoul on September 25.

North Korea now wanted to end the war. Kim said he would accept the old border at the thirty-eighth parallel. The United States and South Korea, however, decided to move on in order to unite Korea under a noncommunist government. MacArthur ordered a "hot pursuit" of the fleeing North Koreans that led UN forces to the Yalu River and the border with China.

In mid-October 1950, General MacArthur met with U.S. president

Harry Truman on Wake Island in the Pacific. MacArthur assured Truman that a massive UN offensive planned for November would conclude the war by Christmas. Despite warnings that China would join the war if the North Koreans were totally defeated, MacArthur believed that his plan to reunify Korea would be a success. He thought that U.S. forces were now strong enough to defeat even the Chinese if they entered the war.

China Enters the War

North Korea is a very mountainous land that gets very cold in winter. In November 1950, just as the fierce North Korean winter was settling in, China launched a massive attack across the border. More than 300,000 Chinese troops overwhelmed the much smaller UN force. A shocked MacArthur told Truman, "We face an entirely new war." MacArthur ordered a retreat in subzero temperatures.

Some troops left by sea, but several U.S. marine and army divisions were trapped inland, surrounded by the Chinese army. They had to fight their way back to the south. The Chinese gave them no time to rest. The U.S. troops froze in the harsh cold. They fought ferociously, killing tens of thousands of Chinese troops. But they could not resist China's overwhelming advance, and they retreated south.

The UN forces were forced to withdraw south of the thirty-eighth parallel once again. In January 1951, they abandoned Seoul for a second time. Then, after a few more months of intense fighting, they held their ground just south of Seoul along the thirty-seventh parallel. MacArthur launched attack after attack, pushing the Chinese and North Koreans back toward the north again. Where the Chinese did not retreat, they were slaughtered. By mid-March, UN forces were able to retake Seoul. Soon, the communists were forced back to the thirty-eighth parallel once more.

The fighting now stalled along the thirty-eighth parallel, with each side mounting ferocious attacks, but neither side able to push the other back. By early spring of 1951, the war had reached a stalemate. Neither side wanted to make the huge and bloody effort to defeat the other side, and both sides seemed willing to accept the prewar border at the thirty-eighth parallel. In June, the Soviet Union told the United States that a **truce** to end the fighting might be possible. The United States then offered to start truce talks. Both North Korea and China accepted the offer.

Talks Begin

Truce talks began on July 10, 1951, at the village of Kaesong. The talks did

Douglas MacArthur (1880–1964)

Douglas MacArthur (*shown left*) was one of the most decorated soldiers in U.S. history and one of the most controversial generals. MacArthur fought in three major wars (World War I, World War II, and the Korean War) and rose to the rank of general of the army, one of only five people to hold that rank in U.S. history.

During World War II MacArthur was the supreme allied commander in the southwest Pacific, where he led a series of military victories over the Japanese. MacArthur formally accepted the Japanese surrender aboard the battleship *Missouri* in Tokyo Bay on September 2, 1945. He was then given the huge responsibility of overseeing the reconstruction and reorganization of occupied Japan. In 1946, MacArthur's staff created the democratic constitution that is still in use in Japan today. The constitution is generally praised as contributing to the stability and prosperity of Japan after the war. He was both beloved and respected by the Japanese people even though he represented an occupying nation.

When the Korean War began, MacArthur was called to halt the North Korean advance, which he did through the daring Incheon landing. When Chinese forces invaded Korea with overwhelming force, MacArthur wanted to strike Manchuria and some Chinese cities with nuclear weapons. President Truman refused MacArthur's request to use the bombs. Angered by Truman's insistence on limiting the war to Korea, MacArthur leaked information to the press, warning of a crushing defeat for U.S. and UN forces if nuclear bombs were not used.

On his own, MacArthur issued a warning to China threatening to expand the war into Chinese territories. Furious, Truman removed MacArthur from his post on April 11, 1951. The popular general returned to the United States and made his final public appearance in a farewell address to a joint session of Congress. He was interrupted by thirty rounds of loud applause. His closing words were: "Old soldiers never die, they just fade away. And like the old soldier of that ballad, I now close my military career and just fade away—an old soldier who tried to do his duty as God gave him the light to see that duty. Good-bye."

General MacArthur died in 1964 at age eighty-four.

not go smoothly. The North Koreans and the Chinese brought up objection after objection to UN cease-fire proposals. In late August, the communists walked out of the talks. Almost immediately, the United States launched a military attack and gained some ground. The defeat brought the North Koreans and Chinese back to the conference table. The peace talks resumed on October 25. On November 27, the talks moved to Panmunjom, a village a few miles away from Kaesong.

At Panmunjom, the talks continued for two more years. The main disagreement was over the future of the tens of thousands of communist prisoners held in camps on Koje Island off the coast of South Korea. The communist negotiators at Panmunjom insisted that all the prisoners be returned to North Korea, but many thousands of the prisoners did not want to return. There were several rebellions at the camps before an agreement was reached through Operation Big Switch in July 1953. Also in 1953, both sides saw a change in leadership. In January, Dwight Eisenhower was sworn in as U.S. president. He threatened to renew the fighting if a truce did not come soon. Then, in March, Soviet leader Joseph Stalin died. Stalin was the generally recognized leader of the communist nations and had strongly influenced the course of the Korean War.

North Korean communist prisoners of war are given food at a camp run by the United Nations on Koje Island in South Korea in March 1952.

United Nations delegates (from left to right) *Major General Howard Turner, Rear Admiral R.E. Liddy, Rear Admiral Arleigh Burke, Major General Lee Hyung Keun, and Vice Admiral C. Turnery Joy leave tents in Panmunjom, South Korea, where they were housed during peace talks to end the Korean War in December 1951.*

The Truce Is Signed

Finally, on July 27, 1953, a truce was signed. It called for both sides to pull back from the battle line. The space between them would become a demilitarized zone. No army could enter the zone without breaking the truce. The truce did not end the war, but the two sides agreed to hold separate peace talks, and the shooting stopped.

Even today, no one is sure exactly how many people died in the Korean War. The U.S. government says that 40,000 American soldiers and 46,000 South Korean soldiers died. Chinese deaths are estimated at more than 400,000, while an estimated 215,000 North Koreans were killed. In all, more than three million people, both soldiers and civilians, are estimated to have lost their lives in the war.

Today, more than sixty years later, a peace agreement officially ending the Korean War has not yet been signed. The demilitarized zone still stretches across the entire width of the Korean Peninsula, and tens of thousands of U.S. and South Korean troops face tens of thousands of North Korean troops across it. For all the hundreds of thousands of lives lost, all the destroyed cities and ruined countryside, the Korean War did not change the post–World War II division of the Korean Peninsula.

CHAPTER 5

The Bumpy Road Ahead

Will the world crisis over North Korea's nuclear weapons come to a peaceful end?

As 2005 ended, there did not seem much hope. Not only were the six-party talks still suspended, but relations between the United States and North Korea, already very bad, actually got worse. During the last few months of 2005, the few remaining official contacts between the United

Soldiers stand guard in front of the inter-Korean industrial park in Kaesong, North Korea, in February 2006. The industrial park is the result of a trade agreement between North Korea and South Korea— South Korean companies built the complex and North Korea provided the labor and land. Consumer goods are produced there for export.

States and North Korea were ended. Programs to recover remains of U.S. war dead from the Korean War, provide food aid to hungry North Koreans, and build nuclear power plants were scrapped. "The official U.S. connections have [dried up]," said Donald Gregg, president of the U.S. Korea Society. The isolation is North Korea's fault, said Christopher Hill, assistant secretary of state for Asia. Once the North Koreans understand that "there's no role for nuclear weapons on the Korean Peninsula," Hill said, "the sooner they will have a brighter future."

"North Korea should become a country accepted by the international community, and to do so, it must first participate in the six-party talks and resolve…nuclear…and other issues," said Japanese chief cabinet secretary Shinzo Abe. "By doing so, North Korea will be accepted by the international community and can rebuild its own economy," he added.

Alleged Criminal Activity

Besides its nuclear program, a major roadblock to any understanding between North Korea and the United States is North Korea's **alleged** criminal activity. North Korean diplomats have been expelled by a number of countries for engaging in criminal activity, including counterfeiting U.S.

At a press conference at the National Assembly in Seoul on February 23, 2006, a lawmaker from the Grand National Party in South Korea holds up a real U.S. hundred-dollar bill and a counterfeit example supposedly made by North Koreans.

currency. Fake $100 bills called "supernotes," produced by North Koreans, are supposed to be the best in the business. They have surfaced in both Japan and Taiwan in recent years. North Korea is also accused of producing fake prescription drugs and U.S. cigarettes, illegally trading in endangered species, illegally selling missiles and other weapons, and laundering money from the illegal drug trade. Money laundering occurs when money from illegal activities is put into a bank and made to appear as if it is the profit of a legitimate transaction. In that way "dirty money" becomes "clean money."

On March 1, 2006, the U.S. State Department said that "it is likely, but not certain, that the North Korean government encourages criminal activities, including narcotics production and trafficking, in order to earn foreign currency for the state and its leaders." The Japanese government believes that a significant amount of the illegal drug methamphetamine that is smuggled into Japan is produced in North Korea. According to a U.S. State Department report, before 2005, "30 percent to 40 percent of methamphetamine seizures in Japan" were linked to North Korea.

According to former U.S. State Department official David Asher, criminal activities—counterfeit money, fake products, and drugs—may now make up as much as 35 to 40 percent of North Korea's exports. The money value of this trade, say U.S. officials, may amount to as much as $1 billion per year. Counterfeiting a country's currency, Asher says, is "an act of economic warfare."

U.S. Sanctions

In the face of alleged criminal activities by North Korea, the Bush administration has imposed economic **sanctions** on Kim Jong-il's country.

An executive order by President Bush in November 2005 froze any North Korean money under U.S. authority. That meant that North Korea could not withdraw or use in any way the money it held in banks under U.S. control. The executive order also banned the sale of products by eight North Korean companies that the United States accuses of selling banned missile, nuclear, or bioweapons technology. At the same time, the United States called upon North Korea to end all its criminal activities, such as counterfeiting and money laundering. South Korea and Japan have joined U.S. sanctions. These sanctions have been effective, crippling North Korea's ability to trade with the outside world and hurting the country's already weak economy. "It's been a huge financial shock—and [North Korea] knows the Americans are on to them and their whole [criminal] network," reported the *Financial Times* of London.

North Korea reacted to the sanctions with anger. It denied that it engages in criminal activity and charged the Bush administration with preparing to attack North Korea. North Korea then withdrew from the six-party talks and cut off any remaining contacts with the United States.

UN food aid for North Korea stopped at the end of 2005 after

In January 2003, North Korea warned its citizens that U.S. sanctions against the country could lead to war. Soon after, thousands gathered to rally in Pyongyang for a stronger military beneath a banner that reads "Attain the Goal with Strong Military!"

North Korea said it no longer needed emergency food shipments, despite concerns that millions of people were still going hungry. North Korea has also been uncomfortable about granting UN aid workers access to the country, because this access runs contrary to North Korea's policy of keeping its 23 million people shielded from outside influence, experts say. At the end of 2005, the Koreans ordered workers from eleven international relief agencies to leave the country. Jan Egeland, the UN emergency relief coordinator, warned that 125,000 North Korean children are now at risk of starving to death.

On January 20, 2006, North Korea accused U.S. secretary of state Condoleezza Rice of making "threatening and blackmailing remarks" after Rice made it clear that the United States was not prepared to lift financial sanctions on North Korea for its alleged counterfeiting and money laundering activities. North Korea has said it will return to the six-party talks involving the United States, China, the two Koreas, Japan, and Russia only if Washington lifts the financial sanctions.

Japan—North Korea Talks

On a more hopeful note, representatives of North Korea and Japan met in February 2006 for the first time in years for talks on improving relations. Two chief sticking points remained: economic assistance for North Korea's sputtering economy and the fate of Japanese citizens who were kidnapped by North Korean agents. In 2002, North Korea admitted that its agents had kidnapped thirteen Japanese citizens in order to force them to train North Korean spies in Japanese language and culture. North Korea later released five of the captives, saying that the other eight were dead. Japan, however, demands proof that the eight are dead. Japan also wants North Korea to answer charges that it has kidnapped other Japanese citizens.

Agreement between Japan and North Korea stalled because of unanswered questions about the kidnapped Japanese and because North Korea demands that Japan pay money to compensate for its colonial rule over Korea between 1910 and 1945.

Hope?

Despite setbacks, all parties have continued to work to get the nuclear talks started again. In January 2006 hope

A unified flag is carried by Korean athletes Bora Lee and Jong-in Lee during the opening ceremonies of the 2006 Winter Olympics in Turin, Italy. The white flag with a blue image of the Korean Peninsula has been carried in previous Olympics, but athletes from North and South Korea compete separately.

for a resolution seemed to come from an unexpected source. On a rare trip outside North Korea to China, Kim Il-sung said that North Korea "would join Chinese comrades in efforts to seek a way of overcoming the difficulties lying in the way of the six-party talks." Yet in another statement, North Korea remained defiant, vowing to keep its nuclear arsenal as a "self-defensive" measure against a possible strike by the United States.

Secretary of State Rice responded, "Our work in the six-party talks is extremely important…and we both urge the North Koreans to come back to the talks without conditions.… North Korea also is being told by the international community that it has to be a Korean peninsula that is free of nuclear weapons and that North Korea must dismantle its nuclear programs."

Progress?

At the end of February and beginning of March 2006, North Korea said for the first time that it was "ready to cooperate in the efforts to settle the issue" of counterfeiting. At the same time, North Korean foreign minister Paek Nam Sun told Russia's Tass news agency that the U.S. allegations were a "conspiracy designed to overthrow the [North Korean government]."

On March 2, North Korean and U.S. officials sat down for discussions about the sanctions. If some agreement can be reached between the United States and North Korea over the sanctions, it would pave the way to begin the six-party talks again.

Meanwhile, North Korea is working to restart a nuclear reactor that would produce enough plutonium to make ten nuclear bombs a year, said Siegfried Hecker, a leading U.S. nuclear scientist. According to the Institute for Science and International Security, a Washington **think tank**, North Korea may have twelve nuclear

FAST FACT

North Korea is one of the most tunneled nations in the world. In 1971 Kim Il-sung ordered tunnels built across the demilitarized zone into South Korea. The zigzag tunnels have doors that lock and seal, air purification units, and places for soldiers to rest. In the case of war, North Korea plans to use the tunnels to transport soldiers behind South Korean and U.S. lines to attack in the rear. Some members of the international community fear that North Korea could plant nuclear bombs in the tunnels to blow up Seoul and other cities in South Korea.

weapons already. Hecker said his main fear is that North Korea's impoverished regime might sell nuclear material to terrorists. "Forty kilograms of plutonium, some number of briefcases anywhere in basements, in one of the 15,000 tunnels in North Korea—nobody will find it," he said.

As other countries try to coax North Korea back to the negotiating table, many experts worry that the clock is ticking. "To whatever extent the North Koreans are proceeding…the absence of progress in the six-party talks means [North Korea is] making further progress towards their increased capability [to produce nuclear weapons of mass destruction]," said John Bolton, the U.S. ambassador to the United Nations. "Time is not on our side."

Time Line

2333 B.C.	According to legend, Korea is founded by King Dangun.
108 B.C.	China conquers the northern part of the Korean Peninsula.
57–18 B.C.	The kingdoms of Silla, Goguryeo, and Baekje are established.
A.D. 668	The Korean Peninsula is unified under the Silla kingdom.
1231	The Mongols invade Korea.
1392–1910	Kings from the Joseon Dynasty rule the Korean peninsula.
1592–1598	Japan invades Korea but is forced out.
1600s	The Manchus invade Korea.
1876	Korea signs a trade treaty with Japan.
1882	Korea signs a trade treaty with the United States.
1910	Japan annexes Korea as a colony.
1919	Koreans rally for independence.
1930s–1945	Koreans are forced to serve in the Japanese military and as laborers in Japan's war effort.
1945–1948	The United States occupies South Korea and the Soviet Union occupies North Korea.
1948	In August, the Republic of Korea is established in the south; in September, the Democratic People's Republic of Korea is established in the north.
1950–1953	The Korean War is fought, ending with a cease-fire.
1970s	South Korea, under dictatorial rule, experiences great economic growth.
1994	Kim Il-sung dies.
1995	More than 2 million North Koreans die in a famine.
2002	In his State of the Union address, President George W. Bush calls North Korea part of an "axis of evil."
2003	North Korea announces its withdrawal from the Nuclear Nonproliferation Treaty and test-fires a missile into the Sea of Japan; North Korea agrees to six-party talks on its nuclear program.
2006	The U.S. State Department accuses North Korea of criminal activities; U.S. and North Korean negotiators meet to discuss U.S. economic sanctions; Kim Jong-il expresses willingness to revive six-nation talks.

Glossary

alleged asserted or suspected, often without complete proof

arsenal all the weapons and military equipment that a country has

Buddhism a major world religion founded by Siddhartha Gautama

cannibalism the practice of humans eating their own dead

command economy an economy in which major decisions are made by the government

communism the belief that all property should be owned in common

concessions agreements to grant something, usually in response to a demand

Confucianism a system of belief and code of behavior for regulating society that was originated in China by Kong Fuzi

dynasty a succession of rulers who belong to the same family

gross national product (GNP) the total monetary value of a nation's goods and services

guerrilla a soldier who does not fight in a regular army unit

hangeul the Korean alphabet

international community the community of nations that are usually in agreement about an issue

Joseon ancient name for Korea

Juche North Korea's philosophy of self-sufficiency

market economy an economy in which major decisions are made by consumers, not the government

Mongols people related to the main population of Mongolia

plutonium a radioactive chemical element produced by refining uranium; the main ingredient in nuclear weapons

reeducation instruction in order to change someone's beliefs

rogue isolated, aberrant, dangerous, uncontrollable

sanctions actions taken by a country or group of countries barring trade or other activity in response to a violation, usually of international law

think tank a research organization that analyzes issues or problems for a government or other institution

truce ending of fighting by mutual agreement

tyranny oppressive and unjust government

For More Information

Books

Behnke, Alison. *North Korea in Pictures.* New York: Lerner, 2004.

Egan, Tracie. *Weapons of Mass Destruction and North Korea.* New York: Rosen, 2004.

Feldman, Ruth. *The Korean War.* New York: Lerner, 2003.

Hill, Valerie. *Korea* (Ask About Asia). Broomall, PA: Mason Crest, 2002.

Web Sites

http://plasma.nationalgeographic.com/mapmachine/profiles/kn.html
Maps and information about North Korea from National Geographic

www.lifeinkorea.com/Culture/spotlight.cfm
A general look at Korean culture and history

www.pbs.org/newshour/forum/august97/korea_8-26.html
Information on the famine in North Korea

www.state.gov/r/pa/ei/bgn/2792.htm
The most up-to-date information about North Korea from the U.S. Department of State Fact Book

Index

About the Author

Charles Piddock is a former editor in chief of Weekly Reader corporation, publisher of sixteen classroom magazines for schools from pre-K through high school, including *Current Events, Current Science,* and *Teen Newsweek.* In his career with Weekly Reader, he has written and edited hundreds of articles for young people of all ages on world and national affairs, science, literature, and other topics. Before working at Weekly Reader, he worked in publishing in New York City and, before that, served as a Peace Corps volunteer in rural West Bengal, India.